LINEATIONS

Other books by Robert Gray:
Creekwater Journal (1974)
Grass Script (1978)
The Skylight (1983)
Selected Poems (1985)
Piano (1988)
Selected Poems (1990); reprinted (1990)
Certain Things (1993)
New and Selected Poems (1995)
Lineations (1996)
New Selected Poems (1998)

Books edited by Robert Gray:
The Younger Australian Poets (1983) with Geoffrey Lehmann
Australian Poetry in the in the Twentieth Century (1991 and 1993)
                                           with Geoffrey Lehmann
Sydney's Poems (1992) with Vivian Smith
Selected Poems of Shaw Neilson (1993)
Drawn from Life: The Journals of John Olsen (1997)

LINEATIONS
ROBERT GRAY

1998

Published by Arc Publications
Nanholme Mill, Shaw Wood Road,
Todmorden, Lancs. OL14 6DA

Copyright © 1998 Robert Gray

Design by Tony Ward
Printed at Arc & Throstle Press
Nanholme Mill, Shaw Wood Road,
Todmorden, Lancs. OL14 6DA

ISBN 1 900072 09 2

The Publishers acknowledge financial assistance from Yorkshire and Humberside Arts.

Arc Publications International Poets
Series Editor: Michael Hulse

Cover picture: *Eucalyptus in Rain* by David Rose

CONTENTS

Currawongs / 9
Harmonica / 12
'The Pines' / 14
Travelling / 16
The Girls / 19
In Thin Air / 20
The Room / 23
A Testimony / 24
The West / 28
Wintry Evenings / 30
Descent / 32
Malthusian Island / 33
Doodling / 38
The White Roads / 40
On South Head / 41
Impromptus / 42
Small Hours / 44
On a Forestry Trail / 45
The Life of a Chinese Poet / 47
Shard / 49
Going Outside / 50
Arrivals and Departures / 51
Illusions / 53
'In one ear . . .' / 56
Afternoon Walk / 57
The Hawkesbury River / 59

The Sideboard / 63
Ritual / 64
The Circus / 65
'Out rowing . . .' / 68
Nambucca Heads / 69
Über Deutschland / 71
Version / 73
A Pine Forest / 74
10 Poems / 76
Acceptance Speech / 78
Passage / 79
Coastline / 81
Impromptus / 82
A Garage / 84
His Muse, to Dylan Thomas / 87
Flight at Dusk / 88
Note / 89
A Sight of Proteus / 90
Isolate Evenings / 95
Beach Shack / 96
Philip Hodgins (1959-1995) / 97
The Sea-Wall / 99
To John Olsen / 102
Wintry Dusk, Bellingen / 105
Epigrams / 106
Sapientia Lachrimarum / 109

ROBERT GRAY was born in 1945. His father owned a banana plantation on the far north coast of New South Wales. Gray attended local schools and then was a journalist on a country newspaper, before moving to Sydney when nineteen. There he has been employed as a journalist, advertising copywriter, mail-sorter, book reviewer, and for the last twenty years as a buyer for bookshops. He has published six collections of poetry, the first in 1974. *Selected Poems* has been through six expanded and revised editions, and is a long-standing text for the final high school examinations in New South Wales.

Gray has won most major literary prizes in Australia; in 1990 he was the youngest winner of the Patrick White Award. He has also received numerous fellowships from the Australia Council, the government arts funding body. Writer-in-residencies he has held include one at Meiji University in Tokyo. At present he is at work on a reminiscence of his father, who was 'a remittance man in his own country'. Apart from writing, his main interest is in painting. He returns regularly to the countryside of the northern New South Wales coast.

CURRAWONGS

Dinner-jacketed, these birds stroll like the mafia, to air
their respectability.
Our acquaintance long made, it seems they've assumed we couldn't care
about amorality.

They'll bring the peeled-looking nestling, to eat it on our clothes wire,
where we have offered them bread;
have often chosen to chuck down here the cellophane wrapper
and the moulded plastic head

of cicadas. One slowly ate a silhouetted grasshopper,
lifting it in a fanfare;
stylised with pride, as though it were holding a broken swastika.
They have tightly brushed-back hair,

snipy Latin features, an expression like a thin moustache,
but the eye is demonized
and belongs more to an African carving, than to an *apache*.
The eye, barely capsulized

in its split pod, has a rind of poisonous yellow around
a blackly-shining, opaque
blight. It is watching every movement in the air, on the ground,
as if it's all a card-stake.

Such birds live more intensely than any gangsters on the run.
Although, at times they deploy
with police cars' confidence — another role they have taken on —
sounding their *calloy, calloy,*

c'loy, a siren, ordering the neighbourhood. On the grass
they appear to strut with arms
slightly akimbo, and with the sense of limited nimbleness,
the stumpiness, and what seems

    *currawong – a larger relative of the magpie
    thongs – flip-flop sandals

the cocky, tilted head, alert for notice, of the bodybuilder.
And then, a pin-pointing beak
is applied quickly, intently, while they stare like a welder.
I noticed one had grown weak,

in the park, below our railing. Through the summer afternoon
it stood drowsily about,
although wary, and when at last the darkness had sifted down
it died, by leaping out,

suddenly, beneath the only headlights in some while on our street,
confused, at the last minute.
That most resonant thump, of something live; and also, I thought,
crunch of bird-twigs. I found it

still breathing, horribly; the beak split wide, and held by a thread,
as happens when wood is splayed,
the eyes squeezed hard, without lashes or tears. It was crash-landed,
crumpled. I ran for a spade;

and answered, 'Don't come,' while disentangling the blade in the dark;
returned, to find it was gone,
and saw two boys, holding something on the far side of the park,
who looked behind as they ran.

God no, I thought — they'll poke about, then toss it into a lane,
soon bored, or over a fence
to a dog, and cackle and run on, already with some new plan. . . .
Those birds are their most intense

 at twilight, in scalloping flight, against the horizon's fire-coal
orange, where it tilts a ramp
onto indigo. They'll strictly show and close the wing's porthole
like a signalman his lamp.

There are some admire them, who admire what remains them in
    us,
who admire the deed, *elan*,
health, affirmation; but now what I see, also, is the pathos
of braggarts and the strong.

At dusk, stepping beneath the drawn latex of vast grey fig trees,
the wolf-whistling currawongs;
or scoring across harbour sails, that are stretched like beer bellies;
above waves' slap, listless as thongs.

HARMONICA

The lamps came on
along the platform, their light as round as dandelion heads
in the sea-mist.

We heard the sea,
from behind a corrugated iron shed, trudging
with Sisyphus tread.

A few of us waited
on that empty stage, way out of town.
The train was late.

There was an Aboriginal; a pair
of old hippies were talking tough in the eighties;
a man and woman arrived, country types.

The town, across the heath,
might have been some lights of a freeway; the road to there
a trickle, in sandy scrub.

The man and woman hardly spoke:
boots, jeans, sheepskin collars; his balding head;
hers the luggage, in plastic bags.

She wore his hat; he'd had a drink.
A middle-aged girl with loose open face, the sort
who might come on a bumpy road.

She waited calmly, in the cold.
He took out and began quietly working on
harmonica, and wasn't bad.

Tapping his boot. A melancholy,
pure and steady, was unwound along the night
a little way.

He knew the great songs, like 'Irene';
the last was 'Amazing Grace'. We'd drawn a bit closer
in the wind.

But kept to the wavering
edges of his tunes. It was private. That sort of thing
hardly happens in an airport lounge.

The train simply appeared, its sound
blown away. A single light, sliding around the forest,
like a satellite out from its planet.

His last address to her
which I could hear, as she stepped up, was the part about
'. . . that saved a wretch

like me. I once was lost, but now I'm found;
was blind,
but now I see.'

'THE PINES'

I went from the town on foot, as seemed fitting for a pilgrimage;
going in the way that we used to, down a white road on the gravel verge.

The sunlight came from amongst the tall eucalyptus with a censer's swing.
Although nearly forty years later, imagining I could find something.

Even now, there were only a few cars, that passed by at a wave.
I arrived before the great wall of pines, and through its black architrave

were the slant paddocks, steaming with weed-tops in the afternoon light.
What I am is that earth, towards the mountains, made animate.

And I found there now a real Hell's Kitchen of the vegetable world —
every kind of trash that grows; lantana and stinking roger run wild;

wolfish leaves with deceiving white hairs, their splintery stings;
blackberry ramping; all the nonsensical, stickily-branching things.

The place had been bulldozed, and grass was overcome, grey and thin,
by farmer's friends (my trousers, the caricature of a bristled chin);

by scrawled plants, equivalents of limpet and slug, in a furtive strife;
things sordid as on a sludgy coastline the cockroachy crustaceous life.

I sat on the ground, among grass plumes, to tell myself the sad story
of the death of a king, although was fitfully dissuaded from being sorry

by a long sceptre of the sunlight that was tilted again towards me;
by glimpsing, amid rabble, the maroon, ivory, and tawny-gold livery

of the true grass of childhood, and through a light golden as Avalon
the hills, still sharp-peaked, as an old log that's been idly hewn.

Below those hills, retracting promontories of eucalypt forest, with a
    seed-head
foliage, mistily, and the tight fleece, hiding the river, clumpy and
    fissured.

I'd hoped to see again the marvellous clouds that accumulate upwards
    there
and make a brilliant Gondal — its every inlet, mountain, and peninsula.

Could anyone have loved a place more than I did this one,
as a fair-haired boy? Beneath the silver-laden tree of the dawn,

within the rotunda of days, the wind-polished immensities of heaven,
amid simmering herbs, plaited water, my spirit was as empty and clean.

It was all physical, I think: not the soul, but the nervous system;
the subtleties of a young animal; and the chosen aloneness, and freedom.

I turned to find the house, going waist-deep toward the Moreton Bay
    fig tree,
its silver blight like photographs of the moon's scars. Only the chimney

showed, of that wreckage, which was wrapped in vines and shooting
    rubbish;
out of bamboo and sour leaves, nettles, and the canes with spines like
    fish.

I'd wandered through many days in that house, confined to a dim
    bedroom,
in daydreams. And could see myself again, a girl to what I have become,

who only wanted to push there, though torn; to find something and
    hack
to my own side, and to kiss those lips, and make my heart awake.

TRAVELLING

High up in the hotel
the sound of traffic, at noon,
troubling
as water left to boil.

•

An early train,
when the streets are washed down.
Office buildings among the clouds, billboards,
blown grass.

•

Telegraph poles, splattered
ink of tree-tops,
and always
the falling
frothy river
of the sky.

•

Wandering late
among a myriad lit
shop windows, with rain
afloat. Those deep
reflections lifting you
onto catwalks.

•

Sunlight comes low
across the bars
of fences, and among
the corn leaves;
it makes a fox terrier pattern
on dirt roads, and is trying
openly
with its final cast

for a fisherman
on the windy river.

•

A whinge of rapid pigeon wings, as
fan-dancing
they descend, out of morning light.
The cornice is a compote
that only wants to rot.

•

On a train, through the long summer evening,
beneath a Wedgwood landscape.
The dark girl's eyes
are lost,
sealed like cowrie shells.

•

All day the clouds: some of them milk
discharged onto a river,
others
timber planed against the grain.

•

On the paddocks, a trudging afternoon —
the smoke disaffections,
shadows claimant.

•

A long walk, which leads to a bare
suburban street,
among empty lots,
where the palings are left to stand
in afternoon storm-light.

•

Below the sandhills
a man goes jogging, on his tough small
reflection, that wriggles
like the heart —
the exuberance
of someone who is treading
his own grapes. The surf
is a mural of Valhalla. A dog, all
wet strings, flaps behind
him, its barking
distant timber thrown down. This
beneath a sky of swept
charcoal, an ocean
in strata
of graphite and silver.

●

Two boys are hanging out
from the cold ladder
of a reservoir
at dusk, and pointing to a heron
that floats away
across the heath, over
the tips of all
the orange grass.
The movement of that bird's wings
is like the waving
of the long grass
in the breeze.

●

From a train, the traveller sees
at first light,
far across the fields, against the foreshortened
slate-blue ocean,
a white lighthouse.

THE GIRLS

All those unbalanced galaxies —
their rivets splayed,
the gas-blue constrictions.

And across the playing fields
lies a blue-white mist
of arc-lamps.

There are girls at practice,
implacable strike
of their hockey sticks,

whose limbs surpass
anything we have contrived
in wood, for shapeliness.

Wandering the pavements,
I watch with the separate men
through wire-netting

the girls play exactly
where they may, within a silent
roaring, and fangs of light.

Nothing seems so marvellous
as a small white ball
exchanged among their sticks.

IN THIN AIR
for Dee

It's songs of you that they play
while I eat alone
the grease of one more café
in an overnight town;

but the arrangements are all made,
the paperwork's done,
and the money has been paid,
so I'm going on —

a swimmer who can't climb
the high stone walls
or a boat ramp, for the slime,
as night falls.

I'll have to go much further
before turning home.
There's kindness of a stranger;
the best is long known.

Icicles, knobbly as candlewax,
that's long on bottles
or hung from candlesticks,
along the hotel lintels,

where I say your name to ingots
on purple night; to steam
above a few houses; to overcoats,
women inside, blown home.

The snow is shapely as meringue,
thousands of miles to come. . . .
I have done such things too long.
Tips of obelisks in foam,

as we came by, were cemeteries;
a river, grey-veined marble;
the mauve, frozen smoke of trees;
snow smothering every gable.

A corruption is waiting hidden,
Conrad somewhere said,
even for affection so freely given
as ours; much is paid.

I lie in the long midnight train.
Thickly, black pinions fly;
we howl in a forest like wolverine.
Dawn's weird chemical sky.

Then most of the day, keeping on
through Canada, I forget
the book I am reading, well begun,
because of looking out —

to wet black trees, snow-sprayed
one side (as if arc-lamp
lit), all of them fraying, then frayed;
to lakes, cold fat on soup;

to a young woman, who was in snow
and steam we'd driven,
standing at nightfall to see us go
at a forest stop, on her own.

Plain houses, of doors and windows;
calcified silos, stables.
Out here, occasional light shows,
early, and warm as waffles.

Morning puts its tongue in the lock,
kisses an iron door, draws away
the lips, leaving blood. How quick
a passion, corroding all the sky. . . .

In the Rockies, one's enthusiastic:
sunsets built of stone.
I thought of that haiku, 'A firefly, look!
Forgetting I was alone.'

There was a waterfall at full stint,
frozen to its rock,
like quartz, or a stroke of paint.
Stopped again, I'm taking stock.

It seems that I've gone far enough
to be offered normal life,
as though flipping over a disc.
I'd never thought to ask.

My life, I imagined, must be a hymn
to the optic nerve.
Other senses, you have proven,
will have all they deserve.

THE ROOM

A round table-top
with a bowl of fruit,
and a black merchant ship

far behind it;
with the peaches' russet nap
and a yellow crescent

lightly speckled.
The cloth's blue and white
diagonals make

a stylized net
of clouds, on this altar
to the Altering —

before the convolvulus
mountains, the
daubed mackerel sky,

the hazy light
of the sidelong bay.
A breeze in here,

as though we heard
a pure note
on the ocean's single string.

A TESTIMONY

Gloomy midnight in spring, rain sinking on the canes in the garden. I
    wanted some ease
from my confusion, and reached out through lamplight for a pen.

I am one of those who have watched their image in the hearth, where a
    fire
was tearing itself into pieces, with its nails and with its fists.

And when shall I lie again in a landscape that is bright like satin
with my Venus of the sweet grass, her breasts as plump as quail?

Shall we sing hymn three six six: 'Art thou weary, art thou sad?' As
    though it matters,
for who are we? Blowing in the abyss, these crying-out shapes of smoke.

The one perfection of this world is lust: is grasping, scheming, longing.
    And entirely of nature,
we're continuous with whatever binds the faceless pebble, that more
    truculently persists.

Along the bladed mountains, and in the deep ravines, flowers come
    forth unknown to men
and pass away unseen. When it is spring there, a thousand bloom. Why
    should this be, and for whom?

Existence must come of itself, and it goes on and on without a reason,
    just because it is.
In human consciousness, it produced an eye. It has arrived where it
    might understand. Perhaps it cannot bear this.

We have envied the crane, her clear bright wings outstretched in fear,
    that flees the dark stormcloud,
seeking a shelter, and to safe shelter, to all her shelter borne.

We have envied when we thought how in the morning light, gently
 outpoured as from a tin,
that awakens Asia's folds, some dusty marauder puts out its claw and
 retakes the earth.

For us, all is whirled away and is vanishing, as though it were the
 sparks of a trampling flame.
Something comes into existence if it coheres with other things; but this
 everlasting fire lives on fire, on all of itself.

Difference, which is loss for us, is the life of matter. And without an
 opposing force, each thing would cease to be.
'Strife is the natural state; it is the source of all. The opposites are in
 agreement, as in a drawn bow.'

The first philosophers were the best, as well as briefest. 'Everything is
 metamorphosis, and nothing can remain.' How could men have
 dreamed
that they would impose their demands upon the nature of this world?

There is a substance to things, which is ungraspable, unbounded;
 divided and passed on, like a secret inheritance; always present,
 in what is always passing, but never found in itself — it both is
 and is not.
Thus matter is profound; is *potentia*. And all that now exists is like the
 surface of the waters.

Things as they are are what is mystical. Those who search deepest are
 returned to life,
to ferns in a jug on the window-ledge, to a burned-off hillslope in the
 dusk that is like an opal.

To a spirited horse, chrysanthemums, a pannikin that drips, creeping
 vines, a cut, the corners
of the mouth, a bedspread, willows, the bowels, shadiness, a lump,
 bright salad, and dust above distant fields.

We are given the surface again, but renewed with awe. And I remember
 what I have to say:
Do not believe those who have promised, in any of their ways, that
 something can be better than the earth.

Although I say this with grief for all of those beings who are like
 shuffling, lumpy birds within a basket,
where they have spent or will spend their lives, and my heart feels
 suddenly stunned.

Again, as in a lit cavern, the headland's crumbling silhouette, the wind's
 emery paper glitter,
the serrations of the bay. And the paddocks, dipping into the sea.

Now a blossom slips through the tall wet boughs that are speckled with
 flowers. Beneath them, and above the hillslope's other trees,
out on the ice-pale harbour, one of the yachts begins its drifting away.

Again, the dog is dancing on the morning dew. This black dog that will
 drape itself like an odalisque
amid the jacaranda's mauve shadow, at noon. That can make us seem a
 sickness of the apes.

What is most needed is that we become more modest. And the work of
 art that can return us to our senses.
Our only paradise is the ordinary: to be fed by what is really here.

Now the sea is dark and harsh as shale. The afternoon storm, a swamp
 growth; sluggish bubbles,
above the whiteness of lawn bowls, on the small town's freshly painted
 green.

Looking out, from a verandah in the forest edge, onto tin roofs, drive-ins,
 supermarkets, fishing boats,
the ocean slopping by the tea-shops, and the coarse cheese-rind of the
 beach.

In the smoky skirts of a brilliant immensity, the headland is sleeping
   like a paw. There, pine trees are shaped as though ink blotted
in the folding of a page. From out of those diffusing hills, an empty wet
   highway's light swallow play.

That road falls to offices and banks, to three spires (with their wrongly-
   directed penitence).
Now, the bunches of the tree-tops are rolling; a white sail has gone.
   Slant rain.

In late afternoon, I read on the verandah, and then look at the clear
   dusk. A striped towel hangs across the rail, beside the banana
   palms.
A single wing on the tall sea is passing the continents of the moon.

THE WEST

The grey sheep are bundles
of grass coiled
and blown tottering, trundled
a little way, in hot wind.

The grass here is born as straw.
Grey-haired bush,
sparse and low, has been scrubbed in
with a tatty brush.

Mostly, there are sticks with hooks,
then stains,
scratches, specks — the flaws
in the weathered canvas of the plains.

We crawl the bottom of a reservoir
that is filled with light *ad infinitum.*
On the salt pan, the light is pure
as milked venom.

One only drives fast through this,
as though with lungs desperate to ascend.
The surface is the narrow strand
of the coastland.

There appear rarely
the improvised strange contraptions
of the trees —
they are like crazy antennae,

standing by the blue tar
of the road, which is full of sky
in long shoals;
or they're land yachts, with riddled sails

of brown or olive-grey,
that lopsidedly blow
toward us; or in a group, they're the shotgun wreck
of an old shanty's fibro.

And the tall leaning silver trucks
with black-goggled faces,
that rupture the sacs of the air,
leave tangled meat as spore —

those Francis Bacon emblems
on the conveyor belt. Their hunger
exhales on the car
as, tall as a clipper or a circus van,

they come floating, then stand
and rush on us like sharks
that leave the sea — out of the mirage's
stylized water,

with their camouflage sheets
abandoned, they strike
right beside us, blind. They are about all
you see here of humankind.

It is a landscape that seems stepping back
through the light, out of what is real,
like the one in a photograph
that was left on a windowsill.

WINTRY EVENINGS

      How beautiful the girls are
of a rainy winter's evening, with legs in warm stockings,
    so tenderly solicitous of themselves:
        small shoulders
      in coats, and the hair brushed out
before leaving work, ceremoniously, upon their shoulders.
  Those legs are like a waterbird's, in quick quick
        transposings
    against lights of the traffic,
stepping silhouetted as though along a causeway, over
    the road that is a dredged lip of molten ore.
      And they pass
    alleys that rot like swamps, that
are dripping with the obscene mantras of rainforests, but
    arrive, a skittering of ballerinas,
        feet swung out,
      safely within this awning.
There is the roundness of a small head above a tweed collar,
   like a bud — one has alighted near, her coat
        lapels stir
      at her breath, crooked fibres
laden with finest dew, as the black, bony tree close by
    a streetlight wears, in its great spiderweb form,
        a springtime
      of crystalline fruit. Traffic
moves like water that's almost level, trickles a little,
    congeals, and gathered nudges itself further
        along this
      avenue, beneath the high-
shouldered forms that it seeks to elude, it seems, amid steam.
    Those monoliths are inlaid with brazen plaques,
        which are here
      tropical cages the young
women sidle beside, their nostrils drawn even finer. They're
    awed by great art, the names within these panes;
        this is to them

discovery rich as parchment.
The girls are lost to us, in the innocent arrogance
   of their pleasure. But before the florist they
      turn again,
   stagey on the pavement, glance
for the bus, with leather satchel strap drawn taut, gripped by
   the small bird of the glove (that is branch-shifting
      and sudden,
   fluttering and alighting
and darting away, among lilt and shrillness). Heads shiny
   as seeds, waists like an otter, the girls with eyes
      dazzled by
   a cogwheel jumble of drizzle
on eyelashes arrive, tilt the heads before chrysanthemums —
   the pensive sweet lolling and the draped limbs of
      their bedspread
   clowns. Although, one sits apart
on the bus stop bench, her gaze adrift in the water at
   her feet, with an empty lap composing the
      Pietà
   of all this dissolving world.
May she, in poor shoes, frail paper boat, never be taken up
   by anyone with hands that are less tender
      than my own.

DESCENT

A white sail that is sharp
as a sabre tip
veers away, beyond the spire
in the headland's shape,

and like a sword is shone,
as the car slips down
towards the bay
of a late afternoon.

It's the sail that's alone
with which I'm taken,
in the back of this car,
sunset coming on —

the one that seems to shun
others' congregation,
although walking there
in the fields of Heaven.

MALTHUSIAN ISLAND

Paradise is always within walls; here it is in the hotel grounds, or around some few great bungalows, with their gardens and pools. Outside, there is wide purgatory.

But within these places one finds a hospital's tenderness in the measuring of a drink. This is done by men of oiled wood, in white skirts stiff as paint: by these simply-whittled men, who can move their limbs without a creak, but whose heads begin to wobble if you speak to them, as though their necks were loose axles. It seems their diffidence, the duffers, their lack of confidence, and it disconcerts, disparages us, who feel we cause it.

They attend a fervid religion in this island — all day, the censer and small bell come to hand, of the cocktails, giving thanks.

There is a melancholy in such heat, when you can do nothing except be waited upon, and yet the sweat runs down like water on sluiced panes, as though it were earned with the hardest work.

And there are the hundreds upon hundreds of crows, that at twilight rise above the old tiles, the Portuguese-style roofs of the town, silently, as if whole bonfires of charred newspaper had burst in the wind.

In the long twilight, a few saris come out to walk on the dusty, closely-grassed walls of the town, which was once a Portuguese, and then a Dutch, and then an English fort: on these brown-blanketed ramparts that overlook the dust-pale, empty sea.

Each woman, as though the Virgin, comes stepping upon a private, unravelling, perpetual small cloud. But she brings her black listless drench of hair, her purple gums, the sphincter-colouring of her mouth, an anxious cunning, her sadly cunning innocence.

There is an English hedgerow tune from the clocktower above the town, on the stifling day's pale, steamy sky. No ironies here, though; no such luxuries. 'This is Paradise,' the old men smile erodedly and say. And with the sun, the deep grime, the damp rot, it does seem, at least, that life here will never end.

'Ah, Paradise,' they tell you, for a few coins, with flies on the cracked lips and on the heavy, beetle-casing eyelids. 'Is it not so, sir?', with much wobbling of the head they say.

The Indian appears to be the emptiest ocean. Over the low wall, while at the roof-top swimming pool, you see the ocean has the pool's colour; with nothing, nothing there; no craft, not even a cloud (maybe a tanker, rarely, just within the horizon). There are usually just the crows, flying near, like a few scouts that openly deploy.

A Hindu lubriciousness is insinuated everywhere: in the decorations on houses and temples; in the shapes of the public buildings, which above the first floor are only ornamental flat façades, of a crumbling poor concrete — everywhere this facile, slippery curvaceousness. Inside, those places are bare, and dank as an old change-room's cement.

At the Catholic cathedral there are Mary and Jesus and open arms and ruby hearts and eyes thrown upwards and neatly combed beards and long sceptres of light. Then, for relief, one finds the Hindus' entirely unsentimental gods, which are as gods would be. For the Hindus, a god is the typhus bacilli; or it is the collector of skulls, that are worn strung on the hips, as dry as gourds: the one who treads with ornate smirk, and an oily pointing of the toe, on a child, that is shrieking the world's great zero.

The Hindu temple has all over it carved figures, in a blurry worn cement, that seem to writhe up there like maggots, in the heat. An almost naked priest shows you inside, down into a urinous damp, and in the dripping darkness holds up his lamp, to the gods in their lairs. These are venomous-looking as snakes in glass cases, or like big cats withdrawn into their pits; and he hisses 'Kali' at your ear in the dark, or 'Ganesh', of the elephant-faced one, with its penis trunk and body like a scrotum, and its sly, slit, mascaraed eyes.

A relief, to visit the educational Buddhists, at their stupa, their Big
   Meringue, that is painted a plastery pink, blue, and white.
   There, you see the vast and bland-faced statue, with its matronly,
   gracious gesture; and murals of people who are always sitting about,
   being taught, in pastels. It is like the socialist version of a Sunday
   school. The Buddha wears light blue robes, a light smile, and his
   figure in the pictures of him reclining for *parinibbana*, for his
   extinction, is propped on one elbow, mildly, like someone who
   watches of an afternoon the children's games. As though it were
   deliberate, this image is the very opposite of a crucifixion. Outside,
   the hopelessness of those lives. Buddhism is the perfection of such
   hopelessness. And yet, which of us will not lose all, whose
   situation not be a hopeless one?

A gardenia petal moon. The sound of a billiard break, amongst the
   moon-soaked pulpy flesh of night. In the garden, frangipani petals
   and giant cockroaches flop onto the warm swimming pool.

Nothing really differs from the days of the Raj. There are the servants
   and the foreign waited-on masters. Except, the foreigners now are
   more idle, and have less involvement. Perhaps they are less well-
   mannered; certainly, they've less style.

In the first smoky-grey light, a few streetlamps still burn, and there is a
   pineapple tone out on the grey sea. All that moves is a dog, nosing
   about in deep shade, where a great tree is lightly blown. Then the
   dog goes on, and of course it is a three-legged one. There is a stir of
   refuse and rot, and the stiff-limbed stroll of a sheet of arse-wiping
   newsprint.

On all the signs, and in the soot-coloured newspapers the Sinhalese
   alphabet teems like spirochaetes. It writhes on the paper money,
   that is turning to mud. Long afterwards, there is a stench in that
   wallet as of filthy socks. Here, money literally stinks.

Standing packed and sweltering in a train, we travel often just metres
   from the sea, with its lightly-fluttered short fringe of foam. There
   are chicken-coop-sized huts, that have rotting grass tops, jostled

wherever there is sand right out upon it. (The people here are almost equally spread all through the island's coastal undergrowth, and the cities are not more notable for their crowds. Everywhere, there is a crowd, or can be. If you stop your taxi on a dirt track in the jungle at night, people materialise all about, within minutes, barefooted, and angular as wood.) From the train you see, crowded down the coast, the long trunks of palm trees, lifting outward from here, like the slightly undulant vapour trails of jets, in a short surge, before the impulse explodes.

The train's sound underneath us is a tangled, thrashing metal. Then it seems to fall into talk about the places that we have seen. Katunayabe, Katunayabe, Trincomalee, Trincomalee, Mannar, Mannar, Chilewa, Mannar, Chilewa, Mannar, Trincomalee, Trincomalee, Belihul, Belihul, Belihul, Mannar, Belihul, Mannar, Belihul, Belihul, Trincomalee, Trincomalee, Trincomalee . . . It is like the rushed and to us easily hysterical syllables of an Indian-style speech.

The heat has produced a continuous sullen smouldering or cloudiness of the light. There is an ubiquitous sickly smell as if spicy food has burned black in the pot. Many of the buildings, together, make mouths full of decayed teeth; or they are flat-faced, low, and give a dull flat look onto the pebbles of the street, among which each day the shallow puddles come and go. And the people are like an acrid black smoke, adrift in the land.

The elephants on the road look so wilted they are each a caricature of someone slumping, in need of a cup of tea. They are led to the filthy river to bathe by young boys who are thin as sticks. You watch an elephant stepping down slowly, one corner at a time, that seems to have painful bandaged legs, and heavily stone-tipped feet; and it stands leaning forward on its trunk, and will only douse itself wearily, a throwaway gesture, with that outhouse liquid, after it has been given many a shout, and clout. Mostly it just stands tilted from the bank, looking down, while the broad sludge turns into a copper screen behind it, and the palms and thatched huts of the other bank are smeared across with the smoky dark. A few tall birds come and sit on poles in the way that each boy sits, who has climbed up with the help of a tail onto his elephant's potato shape, and is now hunched and folded there; and all of them watch how the oxide of the evening is slowly and blindly acting.

A white beach is ablaze in the morning, when we drive down the coast, and is such a pure and empty ellipse that we tell the taxi driver to leave us there and to come back late. The place is only crowded with palm trees, blindly enquiring for the horizon like tentacles. But the water is of blood temperature, and its bright greenness quickly comes to seem like that of a soft drink, it is so sticky. And where we sit down first is beside a coil of human crap. Young men soon come sidling up to sell us coconuts, which they lop the tops from with quick machetes, so that we can drink; and having satisfied a need they move on to dope, and for a time keep on and on, turning the conversation around again to dope, but finally see they must give up, and so then they want to take us to the island in their canoe. But what island is that? There is none. 'Oh yes! Oh yes, sir! There it is, sir!' They point, and we shade our eyes, and see a quarter of a mile out, where the ocean is chrome-plated, a small lengthwise outcrop, very low in the water, of pitted rock. It is crinkled as cold lava, and the colour of rust, and striped all over with bird lime. Their canoe of driftwood is just along from here, tilted on the sand. 'There is the island,' they tell us. 'There it is. Come along, sir.' This is more farcical than a pantomime. We turn away from them, and see the 'island' again, easily now. They are silent, too. There doesn't seem anything we can say.

DOODLING

The rain's
unbottled glut
is cluttering
in the porch's
corner. These
tight and blatherskite
convictions
of the rain.
A pearly fog
above the path's
diagonal
on the saturate
park, and that
sad industry
of crickets
is in recession
once again.
Distant streetlights
tremble, watery
emeralds; the cigar-
bright ember
of a slipping car.
Blue trees
are broad and scoured
like ink-blots;
and, exiled revellers,
each palm,
in bedraggled
feathery head-dress,
is forlorn
as a Fellini
mannequin.
At day's end
still amid desk work,
so the heavy
pile will sidle;

now, however,
I am idle.
There is always,
there is still,
that lit
window, the far
centre
to this one;
as if it were
an ending
to the corridor,
as though
that were here,
within space
and windy time.

THE WHITE ROADS

On the deck
of an old fishing boat

I saw gulls slowly walk
and sparrows hop

that tipped
briefly as a pepper pot,

and far from the dunes
through the galleries

of mulberry trees
of an afternoon

I watched the swallows
roll and float.

ON SOUTH HEAD

The shouts of workmen at football through the twilight
from these wide, elsewhere-empty playing fields
as I walk at their wet perimeter. And the South Head light
again dumps flour on the players, and congeals,

in my head only, their stretching attitudes —
crackles their movements like static — has moved on
above a vague, cement-stiff ocean, while it extrudes
itself, quickly as a cat snatching, on the horizon.

The slingshot trajectory of that snowball flight
compacts into the furthest smoke-wall, without trace;
resumes, stiffly as a white cane, around half the night,
over youths, Laocoön for each other, on this high place,

within a wire fence along the clifftops; swinging over
water-plump lawns, rounded to their brutal deficit;
and, far off, a phantom regiment of rain. Patchy as clover,
the sea below, with mine-deep sounds. In the opposite

direction, a deep elision of the landscape has banked
the city behind the players and a rickety tall goal —
stumps, fire-beaded, on a burned hillslope. This is flanked
by purple cloud and luminous plasma. And lights trail,

a long stream of sparks, amid the city's gouts of light.
Matter dilates or tightens, is a proto-responsiveness;
an intensity; a hubris. A blown rain with blistered sunset.
All that's civilized is pre-ordained in this excess.

IMPROMPTUS

Daylight is dragged from the windows,
calling and gesturing
from further and further off. The bird's cry
a gate closing, on the plains.

ஐ

Butterflies uplifted
above the wet-lipped grotto,
as though uttered by a St Sebastian
skewered with the sun.

ஐ

An old treacle-sweet tune (wrapped on a spoon
quick straps of light). Magpies must be walking about
the farmhouse lawn. And I remember how we came here under
the huge fiery litter of a wintry night.

ஐ

Love long burning,
although ash, remains
a perfume, invincibly
in your hair, these rooms.

ஐ

The porches of the forest are anointed with honey and blood.
In the fields, a fire rubs its hands together. Birds chime
like crystal, and flowers blanch against the lurid wall. No words
for this sky. The world is being held up in the beak of light.

ஐ

In the vast evening, the last of daylight drifts loose
and particulate, like the sugary dust
that is blown off idly from a clear Arab sweet,
and that floats in a room's dim ultramarine.

⁂

There was such moonlight
that we could see him, sitting late
on the hillslope, as though he were expecting
a trapdoor in the lake.

⁂

N.M.G.

It is you have given yourself, a child, to the care
of a stranger, after all of that talk —
you who've gone off so lightly, at a promise,
and have lain down, trusting, hand in hand with the dirt.

SMALL HOURS

I got up early, for the lavatory,
and saw the mottled yard
that was like itself in photocopy
and the moonlight fins on cloud;

then you appeared beside me and
we held a rail as travellers might,
maybe somniloquized, touched a hand,
tried to comprehend the night;

viewed it as though a tasteful grave,
until 'Nice to meet' one of us said,
who turned towards the dark wave
of our fathomless bed.

ON A FORESTRY TRAIL

A choir
of eucalyptus saplings
silvery-grey
soars
for thirty feet or more to where
their diffuse
disassembled leaf-clouds
infiltrate
the light,
and are there not so much like
insects
as harmless clouds
of commas,
or of the closing bracket-mark,
overlapping yet without
growing smudged
or dark;
those leaves are like the finely-curved scratches in the bark
of the saplings'
cool, stone-hard
silvery boles,
the possums' claw-marks,
now in the late afternoon's
thrown-open sky. Behind the leaves
for the moment
there is the faintest blueness,
pale
as watercolour
and yet not
delicate: it is strong with the authority
of a
deputized infinity. And in that sky,
low amongst
the at times almost organ-pipe closeness
of the trees,
there is an actual cloud, long and jutting and in the shape of a loaf,

but of a rich peach tone;
fresh
with the light,
this last easy left-handed gesture of the sun.
At the same time
not far off
the skull of the moon
is here, also, just the cranium,
drifting lightly,
crystalline,
and somehow it is not outdone —
these two
lying together, of an autumn afternoon.
And here, having taken hold among
a regenerated undergrowth
of bitter green —
among the serrated lantana, with its hoops like a barbed wire
defence — the saplings
saunter, drifting down into gullies, to the leaf-mulch inlay of the creeks,
and then out
onto hill-flanks
again, spreading over many acres, in a whispering silvery rain.
I am wandering
through tall grass, the tassel-heads
of paspalum,
along wheeltracks, not much before dark,
where the drawn-out puddles are black
as glass,
having awakened in the shape of a man,
and having a stick with which
to poke,
and an old dog,
and such rare colour
out there beside me; and all of us are
a choir.

THE LIFE OF A CHINESE POET

He was born in Tai-yuan, and lived to see the reign of six different emperors,
and in eighty-nine years wrote five thousand poems, in a rhyming prose or as songs for the *ch'in*.
It could seem that he was old from birth. His life was almost completely uneventful,
except for the always-remembered love that he had for a certain courtesan.
His mother refused to let him marry this girl, who was called Scented Jade,
and soon after he was ordered as a minor clerk to the far province of Fukien.
There he discovered, at times, the consolation of nature — its vividness, and its unthinkable reality.
He writes of the wild mountains, that were sharp and glittering as dog's teeth,
and that could be seen from amongst the hanging flowers of the white lanes.
The river there he also admired, which he says was like the great dragon of Ch'i,
that turned upon itself in all the twelve directions, when subduing the five elements.
It was his dream from youth to take arms against the Golden Tartars,
but the northern frontiers had been made safe; there was no fighting, but only an endless boredom there.
At fifty-four, he went home to his native village, having never gained a preferment,
distressed by what he heard of the luxury and incontinence of the court.
He dreamed in his work of the 'vast smoke' of chariots, as they raced upon the plains;
he described his travels to far outposts, by night on a river that was held within the moon's white stare.
Though he styled himself the Hermit of the Mossy Grove, and said that he was wild, irascible and drunken, it seems he longed for the company of other poets.
He had married a local girl, when she was fifteen, and spent most of his

time quietly lost in his books.
Pondering both the Taoist and Ch'an Buddhist teachings, he grew
    more and more enamoured of nature,
and found his companionship in mountains, flowers, and trees.
In rainy weather he would put aside his studies and trudge to the inn,
    to drink with the farming hands.
'Daily the town inn sells a thousand gallons of wine. The people are
    happy: why should I alone be sad?'
He was utterly sincere in his love of beauty. The thing he has seen
    appears on the white paper. There is a sense of overbrimming life.
A Chinese critic has said, 'His poetry has the simplicity of daily speech;
    in its simplicity there is depth, and in its poignance there is
    tranquillity.'
When he was eighty-one, the Mongols arose once more, and began to
    attack the Celestial Horde;
the armies of the Sung were continually defeated, and were even driven
    out of Szechuan.
Again, he applied for enlistment, but amidst the turmoil in the
    corridors at the provincial capital he was pushed aside and ignored.
Giving up all hope that before he died he would see himself in battle,
    he returned to his village in disgust.
His songs were now being sung by the muleteers in far mountain
    passes, by girls bringing silk to be washed in the streams.
In the capital, they were exclaimed over at wine parties, and were
    murmured beside the Imperial Lake.
He was revered, if rarely seen, in his village, but finally one morning
    the word went around that he had fallen hopelessly ill.
Everything was made ready — the thin coffin, the two thick quilts, and
    the payment for the monks;
the earth was thrown out of his grave onto the hillside, and the incense
    was bought that would smoulder among the graveposts there.
But then, the next day, he rose on his couch, and called for wine to be
    brought him from the marketplace;
he had the blind rolled up on his view to the south, and he wrote some
    impeccable verses, in the tonally-regular, seven-syllable form.

SHARD

One hardly thought,
seeing someone so beautiful and young,
Shall we take

the journey of indignities
together?
Now here we are,

being pressed onwards
and on,
flesh that is easily spoiled

as a pear.
But though my impulse should come
amongst the scaffolding

of Time,
if I think of you, I shall be bound
in desire again.

GOING OUTSIDE

An owl is floating
in a twilight
which has the colours
of grapefruit

painted far along
behind the pines,
those ancient spears
of serrated bone.

The fluttered breast
momentarily lit.
Maybe the dog barks
because of that.

The dog's characterized
on another slope
in misty greenness
where light's draped.

And further along
the dark valley's
damp, amid the chipped
paint of trees,

a car approaches
through severed roots
of the hills, its headlights
vanishing, coming out

on a wound road.
These more bright
than the owl's place
on the after-light.

ARRIVALS AND DEPARTURES

As late as the end of the sixties, the last part of our coming home
was the ten days with P&O, out from Cape Town,

in the most desolate of oceans, that has no islands
or birds or passers-by, and the waters of which are indigo,

almost black, they're so deep. That water is bulldozed by the wind
endlessly. And watching travellers must have known

they were climbing there a mote
in the universe, and have felt the abyss at their backs

hung open; so that often, it is said, someone leapt
into the waiting dark — the turncoat

phenomenon, of wanting to be what you most fear, taking its part.
And the engines' by then almost subliminal thump would stop,

as sailors attempted in some even more frail satellite
to find that person, down the shifting gullies of the sea,

amongst foliage of spray, the ship
become distant, like the day moon — that last intractable bit of gristle —

or an iceberg, sun-struck. And those waiting found silence was added
equal to the depths, as they rolled

with the rail, to watch, amid all the slide, for a head,
which had shown itself to be the darkest thing. Then they would go on

and come to Western Australia, often at dawn, the land
a charcoal line that was putting up light, a clear fume

from old wood; and on those always fumbling, ineffectual fingers of
    salty air
there'd be a smell of bush fires,

the scent of smoke from eucalyptus leaves, so clean
it must have been an exultation to some, that smell

of Australia. And then, the grandeur of their manoeuvrings at the dock,
that played against the voluble spray of birds, and the shine of rooftops,

out in a complex, living air. What fools we are
by the criteria of the senses,

of life. We want to be rid of everything difficult, and give up what
    is real;
as being rid of all that's dark, there is no light.

ILLUSIONS

That humans are a special creation, above the animals.

That the mind can exist separate from the body. (Why then would it need a body?)

That apes in outer space will find a fulfilment there.

That dreams are oracles.

That there is progress in art.

That the evil in human nature is caused by private property.

That abstracted shapes and colours can make an efficient language.

That there have been works of art produced in Hollywood.

That despite their evolving with separate functions, the sexes have in all things equally matched abilities.

That the vanguard party exists in the interests of the working class.

That the Church is required as the intercessor between God and man.

That physical reality, which is always interacting, accruing minute differences, and collapsing into new forms, must be the work of a Creator.

That there is an ultimate simplicity.

That 'if God does not exist, everything is permitted.'

That there must be a God to sanction what we value as morality and beauty.

That it is not actual things we perceive, in their uniqueness and subtlety, and with such surprise, but representations of them only. (As if this distinction could mean something.)

That economics can be a science (rather than its being merely the vagaries of public morale).

That if we create enlightened laws, a bureaucracy will see justice is done.

That the greatest possible happiness and fulfilment for the species lies ahead of us. (It may lie far behind, or just behind.)

That rationality is other than a rationalization of feelings.

That in a perfectly benign society, there will no longer be discontent, dissidence, and revolt.

That there is a truth apart from the pragmatic method of science.

That having denied the artist's conscious meanings and intentions, we can then appreciate the work of art (all of whose formal decisions were based on those intentions).

That this world is other than it shows itself to be.

That because 'they once laughed at the Impressionists', now everything in art that flaunts an innovatory mannerism must be good.

That post-structuralist theory is significant. (All it offers is an attitude of bad faith, and a demonstration that anything can be undermined and destroyed.)

That one should choose between the selfishness and complacency of the political right and the sentimentality and self-righteousness of the left.

That art is for art's sake. (In its sensuousness and its care, art is what Nietzsche says, 'the great stimulus to life'.)

That 'Hamlet and Lear are gay.'

That a rote iconoclasm is the way to truth. (Only that which is held above us can lift us up.)

That art requries theory. (Bad art justifies itself with theory; good art is justified by its immediate sensory appeal.)

That the microscopic is fundamental (as though it exists without the macroscopic).

That 'beauty is only in the eye of the beholder'. (Is vividness, or harmony, or gracefulness?)

That things are one, or that things are many.

That morality is spiritual. (Morality is physiology: the nervous system.)

That love is the reward for friendship. (Friendship is the reward for love.)

That the need to 'make it new' means we must overturn entirely. (Culture is continuity.)

That within the towers of the metropolis, the physical limits of our nature (which are its spiritual limits), as those evolved on the savannah, will no longer apply.

'IN ONE EAR . . .'

In one ear
when she goes out
she'll wear,

being sixteen,
a crystal
from a chandelier,

but here
her face often hangs,
hoping it's unseen,

with a more beautiful
and far
more fierce tear.

AFTERNOON WALK

Now the faintest sparks of rain
have touched my face and arms —
how quickly the storm comes.

It is hung like the foliage
of a wall, half along the sea,
and blows as though dust this way.

The lightning's career is like
discovering a nerve's long root.
A yacht's flame has been put out.

The liner departing, a steep dish
piled with fruit salad of light,
has disappeared in the spilt night.

I go back around the inner slope
of the headland, along a track,
narrowly amid heath and rock.

And rain, slant like sabre cuts,
strikes, as I reach the coral trees;
counters the slow sinuosities.

Leaves spin down, easily as doves,
on the bolt-heads of cobblestone.
Beyond, suburban lights coming on.

Through wet honey-coloured boles
the harbour's clay — mauve and stiff.
I find a ledge beneath the cliff.

Two lovers, in one umbrella,
have come out from somewhere near
and linger kissing, along there.

Close beside me, a taper smoke,
the one drifting woollen strand
of cobweb, afloat on the wind.

It billows, undulant as the boughs,
against all the quivering staves
that mist among architraves.

The rain's crackle and bird-notes
in leaves. Webbed light behind a frieze
of the inter-responding trees.

Leaning here, dry, rain collapses
in me. There is nothing I want back
I've ever known, or that I lack.

THE HAWKESBURY RIVER

All the way out, in the wide estuary, through a cloudy morning light,
to the Caledonian-seeming mountains
that are black
in the sea, the waters are moving shortly upon themselves
with their insect-leg movements — a sawing, gently,
gently.
The entire water
is a slinkily-moving milky silver.

While closer, beneath these high, forest-blackened promontories,
drawn to our left, darkly
as drapes,
are dissolutions of the bank,
big cell-divisions —
the river, in this part, going through its cold repertoire
of Munch-like shapes.

There is hardly a breeze, and we're alone. I can imagine us,
seen from one of the few shacks
embedded here and there
in the eucalyptus slopes, with the curled shape of the jib
borne on this fullness, at the pace
of a leaf, that as yet
is well before the weir.

We left, impelled by first light, from mud-banks in their smoke,
were carried off
like smoke, and reached this empty runway
while it was still reverberant
with the sun,
although utterly quiet.
The only notable sound was the lightly-bounced water
making an applause
beneath our gently tupping
sloop, on finding
it is wood.

Now, through the short day, we two are leaning back into our bodies;
and we cut ourselves bread,
cheese, and fruit,
and pour wine, and watch the broad pelicans alight
on skidding feet,
with their wings of a sudden held up
in cavernous shape,
before they fold neatly as Swiss army knives,
and we idly talk,
in moving back and forth about this wide place, although alert
to every slightest
breeze.

Sometimes, rarely today,
under the steep, rounded hills, that are set deep
in the lake-like water,
with its glass bottle dark —
these hills made up entirely of tight replicas
of their own shape, except where,
in a bowed facade,
there are the occasional sunlit
columns —
sometimes today, below these hills, there has been another yacht;
such purity of form
only matched
by Brancusi's 'Bird in Flight'.

Among the headlands we keep passing, one that we have taken for
    our mark
is a blocked-out sphinx shape —
against its dark flank
single birds
glide, at times, remote as satellites,
blinking and white. Until now, behind one of those, you become aware
the hills are resuming
an older mood.
You see how there is coming upon this place something
more basic (a circling back

within limitation), which is like an encounter with the locked metal
underneath our clothes
and skin.

And as we think of turning home, in the as-yet mild winter afternoon,
the sail flaps
and the wind runs down.
But the long-whiskered sun keeps stalking on, or it is bowled
away like a beach grass, sea-urchin shaped;
it lurches behind the cowls
of the cloaked landscape.

At once, miasmas start to return, floating across the figured dark.
The blocky rubble along the shoreline has already sunk
into night.
The water, where it was for a time striped finely with moving silver,
and interspersed with dots,
complex and fast,
has been erased.
Lying still propped on the hatch-top, I have grown chill,
in all this stretched-apart
downward access
of the dark.
And with nothing that can be done,
I recall,
of a sudden, how my bare wet feet were brushed, back there,
wound, dried,
for a moment — as though in an old dream,
an old
absurdity — with some of the hair
of the sun.

Through a high valley
which is slowly turning around
upon us, that hoves above, blackly, there appears a broken orange yolk,
in coarse strings
across the lesser dark. And the water flaps,
flaps, but can barely move us on — its sound melancholy and hollow

as the dry-blown notes
of an Andean flute.
Though almost becalmed, we are coming athwart
a thin lane
of lit water, that down all of its drawn-out length
is made of little incipient spurts
of light — these
ineffectual, as the motor that is failing
and failing
to ignite.

I have come to stand around now at the bow, so that I can
    watch dwindle,
so I can see
solemnly recede
into the mountain, from where I lean out in the rigging,
what could be
that pale long procession of butter lamps.

THE SIDEBOARD

A car passes at the corner,
the damp street grown silvery and still.
Two of the curtains saunter
beside a shadowy window sill —

the living room, silent as yet,
at my aunts'. As though it's the Ark
of the Covenant, they've set
each treasure, in the semi-dark,

on a sideboard: girls with piper
in a soap-white nude porcelain;
photographs framed in twined silver;
lacquer bowls; a blond manikin;

a butterfly of opal; a plaster
Madonna with plastic tear.
Quietly, as if a cat burglar,
I find out their lost selves in here.

The aunts, one genteel but drunken,
one with only a rat-trap thrill
livening her eyes, have forgotten
about me — gone over the hill

and far away; and I sit on
with old books' caramelised gleam,
light in a tortoise-shell fan,
prickled glass, the cloud's purple dream.

RITUAL

At times a cloud, when you have paused deep in the mountains,
throws its shadow on the upland grass, and this darkness
brought early into the world is like a ferryboat
grounding, that carries a warrior you must confront.
The red gout of a leaf drips from a nearby twig
as though it were flung there. Cicadas are crying
the truth about our lives, with their armour discarded
on dead leaves. Now await you only the long regrets
of the night camp, where your life seems already over
and its sins all that are yours. You grasp, for a moment,
at lines trailing after the birds through the twilight sky
and step forward, into a suddenly steaming void,
as the cloud lifts its hatches. Yellow slopes are swirling.
Right foot and then left foot. Why hesitate, and why grieve?
For you've attained nothing, and so can lose nothing,
not since beginningless time. You have never yet seen
the face of this antagonist, because of a sudden
you strike, with all force, from out of yourself, and are cut
by only a breeze of night. Yet, you hardly can doubt
suave hair was bound quickly in a knot and slung across
a shoulder, and sleeves fell, as those heavy forearms rose.

THE CIRCUS

An old and unregenerate world
is overnight unfurled
on the park — something from the fifties
and from the medieval centuries;
it has changed less than the Church
and comes to smutch
a wealthy reserve, beside the yacht club and tennis court.
I'm walking late
when the circus arrives here, through our liberals' confusion.
It's without flambeaux: the power generation
is on a truck. Those spatulate shadows, in the foggy night,
unload at the point, in blue light.
A ring-in myself, I have to go
around there, on the empty harbour-front walk; and I see someone throw,
at once, a huge grey tongue,
with other offal, upon the grass — it dangles its string
as if a bouquet
that's been ordered for a Salomé.
The caravans are parking anywhere, with their backs to the harbour,
now after midnight, and hunger
makes the tiger shout
in the shadows, pacing out
four strides, and then back — dreadful to watch
the rapid tension of this match,
so dripping and furious.
Someone comes staggering towards it already, solicitous
with a sloppy tub
full of snake-tunnelled hearts and of watery blood.
Car lights, behind a dark colonnade
of great Moreton Bay fig trees, back by the road,
appear and disappear, like coins dropped
into a pool, where the water's slopped
and clears, rapidly and intermittently — those people drifting unaware
of the forthrightness here.
I'm back soon after dawn,
and the workers are out already, also unshaven.

True, at this hour, that the creases
in the men's looks make furtive and bitter places.
They've teeth missing, and they smoke and spit,
and are ravaged or overweight.
People have lined up with buckets at a tap
and portable toilets are set up
beyond the laid-out small tents. I'm surprised to see
a huddle of dwarfs. One comes straight across to me, truculently,
glares out of his squashed shape,
the legs buckled, and with his hair in a 'flat top',
and tells me to piss off; then he strides
back, ignoring the duckboards.
His brow is pressed into a deep crease, beneath its curlicue,
and his wide-splayed legs,
from behind him, are worked like an African canoe,
where one digs
either side, heavily, to row.
Such curiosity of mine is thoughtless, I know.
A foetid smell of steamy green piss
and of soaked straw and dung hangs over all this.
I walk toward the morse code, jubilant water.
Here they have sat, wrapped up, sinking toward his centre,
nodding, one of their old men.
Life shows this kindness to some, in getting them ready for oblivion.
The harbour's all the stardust and spangles
around here, but hard to ignore the circus, as it steps from its tangles,
the tent rising like a gown. I cross to the elephants, having seen
two accidentally bump and begin a routine,
a soft shoe, in slow motion,
swaying weightlessly, like plants underneath the ocean.
Then each is once more inert,
as though dangled from a crane. They'll scuff the padded foot
occasionally, and scatter chaff
in a throw-away gesture, that is like a hollow laugh.
Every inch of them is cross-scored and dried
as palings, weathered
among the sand dunes. They're clothed in tarpaulins,
loose-fitting as tendons

of an old man's throat. Skinny girls have come out, whose skin
is almost neon white. One hangs a lurid washing, and they lean
on guy-ropes, a moment, in the sun.
(A baby that's tripped in the mud is a nuisance and no-one's armful.)
They're dressed for rehearsal
in scanty fishnet tights, drawn high on their loins,
and are loose yet sinewed. Paltry as coins,
it might seem, but they have the discipline of their artistry,
as well as whatever cliché
they share with us, of longing and hurt.
The big cats are driven out
of their cages, into the tent — the carts drawn up like a tail,
and the animals, goaded on, trail
well apart, from door to open door, then down a wire tunnel,
crouching, as into a funnel,
so that they burst forth, surging upwards impressively
within. The tiger's last, and runs the cages' full length directly,
low-slung, swift as a train engine
when unencumbered, treading each piston.
It can move fast as a wasp does in attack.
One hears a whip or pistol crack
inside. The male lion, with big grassy head-dress and shrunken stem,
went with heavy clearing of phlegm;
meditative, resentful. An emblematic flower,
wilting. It is toothless, no doubt, but like Baudelaire's the rancour
of the sideways looks,
to remind us about the rumour of a swordstick, of its gloveful of
    hooks.
Leaving, I see the old man
is dozing on. Set for a lookout, this graduand
has nothing to tell us. Except, to make us hope that we perform
as calmly, in the face of final harm.
I look back and there is an elephant
being hosed, that's lambent;
and I wait a few minutes, to see if it wears for a hat
the morning's first crisp yacht.

'OUT ROWING . . .'

Out rowing at night
on the river

voices

in the stillness
some cabins

among

the shoreline
in one

a bottle is opened

any of those might be
a lantern

that I could hold

NAMBUCCA HEADS

Shaped like a 'lady's finger',
a biscuit-coloured sandbar;
the estuary is blue china.

Behind the dunes are swamp oak;
amongst them, a tin-roof shack
with a rolled sail of beige smoke.

The nearest navy-blue mountain
is fluted like a blown curtain.
On summer afternoons the rain

slops, big as white grapes each drop,
for an hour. A rowboat drawn up
by the shack's tomato crop,

and the collapsing fence is
under passionfruit vines like sheaves.
Amid the cabbages, rain seethes.

A fig tree above the river,
the inland side, will grow circular
at dusk. There, cattle wander

the flat bronze paddocks. Tall poles
in haze, to the smoke-blue hills.
By the coast, eucalyptus-shoals —

this foliage is like dolphins;
rolling shapes, and leaping ones
in places. Close-packed, it shines

with a salt spray of light. Strung
from headlands, the beaches are long
bows — glisten of vibrant string.

Out on the river's great billow
comes the train, that is trundled slow
on metal trestles, with below,

more loosely, the white pelicans.
Leaning in his shack, an old man's
waved. Then, as each iron roof shines,

a slant, strewn town's revealed. Whether
dawn or dusk, it chimes silver,
as in tall rain. Here the river,

on humid-fleshed nights, sways sequins;
ophidian-dark. And neon's
red mist, on the veal-pink dawns.

Still this flaked ocean, blazing like
a furnace, after a night's work,
breathes mildness. O white Pacific.

ÜBER DEUTSCHLAND

Outside the tall hotel's
windows, of a sudden,
appears an unwinding
belated snow, the big

shreds loosely-fleshed, tatty.
These guttural, thickly-
uttered, wet syllables
of a stumbling snow. All

of it suggesting the
bitterest outcome for
a letter, that is cast
out, exploded. We're at

the beginning of spring
and here's a redundant
and long over-ripe snow.
But in the dim cinema

of our room, it is we
are carried down, sinking
steadily, in a long
pan, we who seem settling

directly, as in a goods
lift, through such various
up-draughts, lateral drifts,
vortices, and flurries.

The thick veil of 'atoms
in the void' slackens now
briefly and secretly
and shows within itself

one floating edifice —
beer hall or hunting lodge.
We go out, to dispel,
perhaps, the sinking; to

snow that is put out as
embers are at night, in
touching us. And find a
bit of jollity, a bit

of quick-stepping, as beer-
bellies remove, mincing
and raucous, indoors. The
Germans are like the Church

and being nice, these days.
Over cake shop, laundromat,
there arises, fascistic,
iron-black, and bristling, a

cathedral — silhouette
of the Gothic forest.
About its spires, along
the alley of building-tops,

furiously, the low clouds
are carried on, unrelieved:
racing and entwining like
cords of an icy, slush-

thickened water; undulant,
spilling, hurtling towards
circumstance. These whirling
wings of the locust horde.

VERSION

With my face pressed all day against the glass
we crossed a distant plain;
I watched how the steppes were heavily drawn past
from the smoky train.

And saw clouds and rivers slipping away, too,
hills fold and unfold.
Adrift on the earth, what is it that keeps you?
What is it we can hold?

In the glass, I watched her face that mornings made
glow amber as honey,
and noon simmered olive oil in colonnades
among pines' greenery.

Paused at night, heard a fog horn on the harbour
as a ship left the earth.
This when I'd forgotten not to remember.
I would have liked a berth.

All one has might as well be water dangling
where birds light upon
the boughs – of a sudden, there has come a wing
and it's shattered and gone.

What we are is this pressure, that's not our own;
unrelieved, redeployed.
It will pulse and congeal in the dark again
when all worlds are destroyed.

A PINE FOREST

In autumn windows, evening's land
of ebony and fire. Out there stand
the pines, shingled on the valley;
and cold rises off them early,
exhaled across the axe-carved hills.
Above this now, a liquor swirls
in the clear glass of dusk, that's lit
already with a small starlight
for highlights — the fiery water
is brandished, reflects a grandeur
beyond here, or a roaring wassail,
most likely, chaotic, brutal.
These pines that I gaze on arouse
disquiet in me. In early hours,
while staying here, I walk among them,
every day in a damp chasm,
a gloom. Insurgent in this country,
they're alien. 'The Ghost of a Flea',
Blake's drawing of his monstrous vision,
comes to mind. On television
one saw the origin of this trope —
they showed within a microscope
demonic fleas, and other mites.
The quiet trees recall such parasites
for me. (And are, in their tight band,
too dark, too military, in a land
that naturally wears the various,
airy, open eucalyptus —
those more casual, improvised things;
each floating its kites, on many strings.)
Under the pines, heavy needles
seem insect droppings and dead cells
coating a nest; the spiked antlers
and broken teeth, struggling creatures'
armoury; and the plated boles,
bristling, moss-infected, are scales.

Such life pronounces too gloweringly
that it's survival machinery.
Seen afar, sluggish in midday smoke,
the history that the trees evoke,
matted, and drawn into a mass,
is horrible, insalubrious.
(I think of great war paintings by Dix
that one can't love, but one respects.)
The light is a fire, just too far
away for harm, set where we are.

10 POEMS

I sit and watch
the way that rain is falling,
its eyes closed.

As if one dead
had laid an arm around
your shoulders, wintry sun.

After a quarrel
she makes love in the shower
to the limbs of water.

A shell thrown out
by the ocean drives onwards
to infinity.

The crows go over
all day, back and forth, anxious
to lace night with night.

Writing beneath vines;
a Sunday. The slow, clean strokes
of the cricket match.

Bring my mother in
from the morning, she will vanish
in that light.

The distant train
flows like a headlong bike race,
splashing gulls. Late sun.

In the vase, flowers
from deep in the heathland
open their eyes.

The shadowy sides
of everything, on the way down
to the white sea.

ACCEPTANCE SPEECH

Stopping in the tangle
of a garden, in the early morning, amongst its frettings,
dangles,
and overlays, I have disappeared
for a moment, in a fragrance.

It was as if it were the light which knew the light
on the overwhelmed grass;
as though
it were itself that smelled the dampness
in this perfume.

The damp air, which came thinly from off the dead leaves
and the reeds,
Hermes.
As when a breast is turned in the hand, some further minute degree,
a mouth opens, the pure waters fall.

Such an acceptance, as in that moment, accepts all that is
as indivisible; sees it is dependent
on everything in time.
It is this which you did not understand
in all your other lives.

PASSAGE

The train is long and slow
and curves away
as though
one saw upon a leaf
the detour of a worm

it is dragging between
the lilies
white
and flagrant
outside the bedroom

each bloom
in the green light
is filled with rain
a syrup
in a tall stirrup cup

and the mosquito it would seem
this bit of soul
this little grey appetite
would like to stamp
its fibrils

upon the air
the way that it keeps pacing
tightly and frustrated
wavering and drawn
tracing

a freely-treated shape
it wants
hovering something of that drink
while the train
that rattled the stony panes

near sundown
and the sunlight drawn straight
a wet blond
across the forest top
are gone

in the time that it has taken
for the windows to be shut.

COASTLINE

A burned caramel sky to westward
for a sunset
above the lights of the towns
in a thin rain.

The thistle-tops of the headlights
are refrigerator blue,
along a curving highway, under
the broken range.

An ocean, that wears grey gauze,
collapses like a lung
upon the beach. A black dog is searching
by the sad wall.

Beneath dark shelves of the pine trees,
deep in the wetness
of a garden, there are white curtains
that might be columns.

Aisles and arcades, all deserted, except
for people with rags
tied about them. The flame lit here to some effect
is above the refinery.

And neon keeps on with its performance
as wearily
as a cocktail waitress. We climb from the town
into a washed twilight.

The star that is now wriggling there
like a crook'd finger
has a maliciousness, it would seem,
that is very old.

IMPROMPTUS

Moonlit night; the willows
have drawn their curtains. A calm
on the face of the main street. A shadow
takes a shadow's hand.

&

A moth at nightfall grabs the porch light
like a man drowning on a slippery buoy. Shutters clash,
sand trickles out of the wall. A lemon tree has inclined
to the long curlicued whisperings of the dust.

&

In the new suburbs, in light rain,
at the road's verge treading its line
with the stateliness of a tightrope walker,
it might seem, the diesel roller.

&

On wet sand, a dog goes trotting, way ahead;
the spume is blown across his plume.
He doesn't look back, and so neither do I,
and we will be quenched in the dark.

&

Under a cliff, stones
in sea-mist, and a stag's bones
caging a butterfly, hung
blackly as blood and fluttering.

&

Still with my head lowered
at the desk, I hear
the stream again.
Is it golden now, or violet?

❧

To find a room within the waves,
a lamp of honey, beneath the salt. . . .
The wet lianas are ascending
through the lightning, at night.

A GARAGE

In one of the side streets
of a small hot town
off the highway

I noticed the garage,
its white boards peeling
among the grey paling fences.

There was a lone petrol pump,
from the sixties, perhaps,
out in the sun-blaze.

With its human scale
and humanoid appearance
this had a presence —

it seemed the man-servant
of our adventures on the road,
the doorman of our chances.

We pulled in, for nostalgia,
onto concrete. From where
did this thing's subtle

almost avoidable sense
of sacrifice and remorse
arise? One could feel it

as though it were a line held
in the hand, drifted far out
somewhere, unweighted.

Who was this, in weathered
blue outfit, with badge,
expressionless small head,

and rubbery arm across
to its shoulder, either dutifully
or out of diffidence?

Was it presenting arms, and in
servitude or willingness?
Such stoicism discomforts,

implies a threat, and rebellion.
Elusive as music, our feelings
are blown through us. How

to interpret them? — Some person
dependable but dangerous,
solicitous and sinister. I looked off

down a blank street, of pines,
telegraph poles, old houses
in deep yards, that made

a genuflection, in approaching
gentian hills. And then into
the garage, a long dark

barn, an empty corridor
in the galaxy, with somewhere
far along it one star

crackling and flaring
bluely. And then at the black
dog, in its narrow shade.

And at the old bowser —
a feeling still proclaimed and
ungraspable, in the light.

Someone had shouted
acknowledgement, and so we sat
quietly there. The light

had become an interest
of this place, pronounced
by contrast with the peculiar

matt blackness of sump-oil
stains, widely soaked
into earth, gravel, and cement.

A blackness that was opaque
as the diversions
of the tunnelling heart.

HIS MUSE, TO DYLAN THOMAS

'If I were tickled by the rub of love . . .',
if I was tickled by the rubber glove,
excuse me, doctor. That was not love.

FLIGHT AT DUSK

At eighteen thousand feet we have come
into the presence of a storm
that is purplish-black. Like an oak, and then pine,
this flared shape. The vast trunk is rain.
Yggdrasil, with roots in Hell,
its boughs through Heaven, in reversal —
Hell is a synonym of falling,
ventured on here; the rain is blessing
the ground. Far beneath, dustily,
what had seemed a landscape seen indistinctly
is only cloud. Streaming cobwebs.
All over this tree, lightning stabs;
a twitching, darting — it's the constant strife
and nerves of insect and bird life.
Unlike Satan, we are coasting
the walls of Darkness. On our western wing
we lean, too, and despondently
we sink. — A mosquito, so minutely.
The wind has shifted: there is no chance to run
from such nuclear explosion —
as though stepping on ice, our small craft
lurches, dithers, in just the draught.
(At dusk, the owl of Minerva's flight
has begun, that brings us insight.)
I turn to incomplete work
spread on my lap. When next I look
the moon I had seen, a fine bowl dripping
one star, where it tilted, is vanishing,
and the stripe of ultramarine, lit
like an ad for a Turkish sweet.
I feel, though I keep on working here carefully,
disgust. So passive, so arbitrary.

NOTE

It has always seemed to me that natural things would help us
if only we could hear
the eloquence
of their dumb ministry.

What is it that these things of the world do?
They submit,
and they endure.
They flourish. They don't ask for anything.

They simply take what is given.
They flourish,
all at once, where it had seemed they were merely enduring.
Everything can touch them.

We are searching for the world, amongst this diversity
of existence,
that has formed itself so loosely
in a ramshackle system.

While our lives, one can see, are just a routine sacrifice,
consumed and forgotten,
off somewhere to one corner
in the courts of the sun.

What can last? Only what we have made
and hand on
amongst ourselves, that is withering in our hands,
but never known without us.

So we take the dark roads
in beautiful clothing, greeting each other;
sorry for the void
that cannot see what we've become.

A SIGHT OF PROTEUS
For Ted and Kathy Hillyer

These squat or long-drawn shapes, like toadstool caps,
are sandstone rocks
in silhouette, against a silvery band of ocean
of an afternoon,

as I climb down from the track along the cliff-tops
and pause, on opportunistic steps,
above gravel
in the shingle pits,

that lie below those ramparts on the wide rock tables;
where you can walk
at eye-level
with the running-in of the surf. I look back

along the cliff-face, its facets
grey and fissured
as a Picasso, cubist period,
and see how the bushfire-swift, white surfline ignites

and drives smoke
toward shore, while the sea out from here is a deep navy,
past where the sun props
one arm behind it, and is calm and empty.

Below, the waves dragging off the black rock platform
are a stark root-system,
or a backward-sucked lightning screen,
pronged, a few moments, in relative slow-motion.

Awaiting me, obliquely, is a deserted beach, and those wisps
of she-oak, that complain
delicately, it seems, behind it; and on the low dunes
are beach vines

and the aqua-coloured grass, that leans
onto any breeze,
as compliant as shadows.
The light in the wet shore has a metallic sheen

as if great ventilator shafts
are sunken there. And one can see — braced on the rocks of this corner,
in hope of dolphins —
how the river flatly drifts

parallel with the dunes, and has sand
banked shining within it, and how the mangrove island
is all white birds,
settled there like the chips of light on part of the water.

This river as slowly as possible comes around
to its estuary. The town,
under the headland's smooth grass haunch and the reservoir,
is the poles for light and telephone,

a block of wooden flats (which I know says Vacancy),
the steep roofs of pub and general store,
a cross, the signs on the hamburger and video joints, and the fibro
or timber houses, climbing from their hollow

with the climbing bitumen,
onto a cleared and scrubby hillside.
The mountains, far beyond, are drawn to left and right,
and their flat facade

is transient
as convolvulus, in colour,
and this affects their form, and their locality,
or it does seemingly.

Earlier, when setting out,
I saw a girl from town run down the shore,
passing her clothes to a friend, and, coiling up her black hair
one-handed, at the last moment,

dive beneath a wave. She swam
easily to where some boardriders had settled in the sun,
then lay back among them,
talking, tilted in the sea that passed,

her body white through the clear surface of those rollers,
the bikini-bottom like a shadow;
and only now
she returns, with the other kids, striding back strongly onto shore.

Sometimes the fishermen work from down there,
using a great net
immemorial style: wading out, while two undo it from a rowing boat
that is the last of its floats,

and they take the catch right at their front door.
They draw
a broad welcoming one-armed embrace upon the water
that turns crushing.

I saw them do this toward evening, as the few boardriders came home,
who rode above the net-hem,
hot-dogging and stylish; and the men, hanging on,
shouted at them,

calling someone a young bastard;
one probably his father.
Some women, sometimes, and other men
from the pub, each of those holding a glass or a beer can,

come and sit in the dunes,
but not much chiacking goes on, as the surf totters
the older workers, thigh-deep, who take the strain, and cuffs the others
in their faces.

They know when a school of fish is about to pass this town
by a fire a lookout will set
a match to, on top of the headland
beneath which I stand. That sight

brings them running from the pub,
while others drive, and hauling their net from a trailer,
carrying it in file —
it is dark as the seaweed along the shore, in its roll.

And when they pick
the fish they want, there on the beach, they pack
these in plastic
and ice, and onto the four-wheel drives, backed up;

which, to an aesthete watching,
is a pity, particularly
the carving-up of the shore; and then they race back
to a cold-room shed, near the railway.

With twilight, the long prow of tumbled-down rock
before this headland
is surrounded by an almost luminescent
foam, constantly elastic;

and a loose breast-pocket handkerchief of whiteness
appears, against black stone,
from time to time, with a notable flourish, and is being re-tucked
as you look again.

Out to sea, the water's become
a rich greenish-grey, oil-streaked it would seem
with violet, and the sky
a dark violet-grey.

And there is something extraordinary sailing by —
an arctic cloud,
shelved and squared, and upreared out of the horizon,
lit from far inland, where the sun has almost disappeared;

blue, apricot and rose veils shifting within its white.
Though, such a sight
fades very soon: the power turned off, it loses splendour and form
as you watch.

And now the low black mountain rim
is gilt-fringed
far along, with the light that has been hived here, progressively,
in the surf, and sealed away.

There's a last surfrider, just there,
and another one, moving from beyond some rocks;
each in the mild air still waiting astride
his board,

although it's invisible, from where I look down.
They seem, in drifting clear
of the shadows, to be giants, who are standing out
amid the sea's tremor, those myriad oil-cups of low blue light.

The closest one, an old hippie, is bald, with a flag-like beard
and a carved build, and he folds his arms
like a Greek sea-god,
who looks in across that blowing hem

to the flimsy town. No longer hidden,
he is considering going ashore, or he longs to, and living in this place
so 'backward' and 'slow',
where the smoky streetlights have come on.

ISOLATE EVENINGS

The Japanese ink, moist on the stone —
stroking a moonlit pelt,
or it is blackest wine.

A subtle carbon perfume to this tablet
being worked. It is a joyful
accumulation, towards sleep.

BEACH SHACK

It's wisteria-grown, but I
push back the gritty, cracked window,
just arrived. The usual storm,
soon. Grass looks withered, even so.

A slanted fence, where magpies fall.
The east is tar, paint-slapped thickly,
and the scalloped surf keeps passing
along the heads, radiantly.

At most times drab, now the other
white places on this slope throw back
a light that's granular, over-proof.
Broken pickets, then water's black,

on which the foam rises and soars
to land, ablaze in its spread flight.
About the yard amble warbling
those magpies, closed in black and white.

PHILIP HODGINS (1959-1995)

Your funeral recalled for me your poems;
I seemed to feel your touch about it all —
sparse trees nearby, sinuous, stringy gums,
their leaves, rags on barbed wire; the lustrous call
of furious magpies; clay instead of tombs;
and low weather, with dry weeds and thistle
that we came wandering over, scatteredly,
to the coffin, strung above its cavity.

The empty place the world is hung upon.
'No speeches, only verse,' in your dicta.
I read one of those pieces you had chosen,
'Sailing to Byzantium'. How bitter
the humour, the irony, you'd added. Then,
because there'd dried up here part of the delta
of the Murray, it seemed right that Les spoke —
spontaneously brilliant, a common bloke.

Hartley and Paul read briefly. That was all.
Backyards of wooden houses, fairly near.
Each of us threw into the eight-foot hole
a flower. But first, had to stand and hear
ropes slowly creak, unwound from a steel rail —
a labour to breathe, stopping; heads bowed there.
At a mullock heap, along that gravel track,
out in Victoria, something gold put back.

Just nights before your twelve-year fight was up
you rang. 'Tell them I was a great hater,'
you said. The Literature Board's lucky-dip,
demoralising to a true writer;
feminists' self-pitying career; French slop,
that only 'signs' exist (hearts of water);
treasonous clerks in the university . . .
condemning these you'd call your best elegy.

You were as loyal as a classic Roman;
vehement and pure; a believer in style;
stoic, yet glamorous like Wilfred Owen;
the exemplar of an Australian school —
going straight for the pay-dirt of emotion,
laconic, pragmatic and sceptical.
'Live another thirty years!' If I do,
it'll seem a moment, then. I'll think of you.

THE SEA-WALL

The headland has been raided,
eaten, broken away —
a carcass that hyenas
have found. It is the quarry

for the wall, this drawn-forth
rough intestine of stone;
a tight jumble of shapes like
DNA or protein.

Among these, a concrete path
goes nowhere, to carry
with bold gesture to sea
just tracks of the railway

that built it (now rust flakes
and the sleeper's imprint).
Tipped each side, more recent,
are huge blocks of cement.

What purpose the wall served
has been lost (apart from
that of swimmers and paddlers).
Now, no ships ever come.

On the wall, looking back past
broken edge and sharp angle,
the line of the headland
holds this concrete and shale

beneath an undulent
stroke of grass, like green fur,
against blue panes of stone.
The air's a mode of fire.

I've seen the wall at dawn
from that grass: in silhouette,
a stamen weighed with seed,
on the sea's milky-white.

People come there early
and sit on flat roof-tops
of their small, skewed pueblo
that they drape with bright stripes.

And here they weed the garden
of the sea, in alcoves,
or snorkel above rocks,
and laugh when ocean shoves

heavily — a whale, with spume —
the outside curve. They cover
just eyes and genitals,
organs of too much pleasure.

About them, soap flakes sprinkled,
then higher on the sea
soap powder, then lathered clouds,
or the whole crisp laundry.

Children come cycling by,
and men scrape fish they've caught;
a woman's on the ocean
with a red towel drawn straight

behind her, which she levers
slowly back and forth; her breasts
solemnly eye those passing;
the finest sea-spray floats

in hair on forearms, on
a girl's lip; feet are slapped
through puddles; in long chevrons
of shade, picnics unpacked.

The sea's striped purple, blue-green
and chrome. An idle yacht;
a black dog against its shape,
on a pedestal, alert.

Slightly-curved, like fishing rods,
this wall unfailingly
sprouts its riffled sparse hairs,
especially on Sunday.

TO JOHN OLSEN

On your workbench were scattered some goose quills,
beside broken charcoal, inky bottles,
one unused. This, a sill of twig-brushed snow,
or smoothly threaded white sand, when the flow
of ocean's edge has left a glaze revealed.
With licked fringe, all fibres perfectly sealed,
buoyant and raked, resting at quiff and horn,
this line, as you noticed, had your guest drawn.
You trimmed its tip, to demonstrate for me
the calligraphic possibility
in such an implement. Not when it flew
was it more supplely used; and it grew
in stature, out of your fist. The winged grip
put wings to your mind — every surge, each dip,
of mountains, ranging far off, were caressed
by your gaze, ink proved, their space possessed.
I tried it. Perfect balance in the hand;
the hollow spine weighed by the air it fanned.
This not designed, except through increments
of spontaneous change, by accidents,
that breed, when used opportunistically.
I thought, too, Red Indians' dignity
was conferred upon them by the eagle
feathers they gathered — how not be regal
and alert, underneath those crowns they wore.
I glimpsed this, while you urged me on to draw;
and dipping with that heroic billow,
traced the bleached draperies outside Lithgow.
'Look at that,' you cried, and presented me
the instrument for such discovery.
I wanted them to continue to ply
this great quill, felt imperious as Bligh,
possessed by a sagacity like Cook's,
but there was more to learn — turned to your works,
and found amongst them their diversity.
I admired a more languid quality

in your brushwork; so Aboriginal,
its ease, its slowness; this the very style
of our impassive land: like campfire smoke,
eucalypt boughs, shorelines, creeks. You evoke
a Chinese spirit, too — the passive strengths,
so awesome, of earth and water. Those great lengths
your lines sustain are time, then timelessness.
How Taoist, the reins you give to looseness,
and tauten, just where you need. You've the skills
that suit this place. Your marks become tendrils
of waterlilies, inky waterholes,
the fur of caterpillars, the great boles,
slowly surging, of gum trees, scribbled knots
of foliage, speckled pond-life, mallee roots.
These trails, watery or tarred, are aerial
(native again): concepts, yet sensual.
Starting with *art brut*, the fashion once, you
acclimatised it — had this land strike through.
Your project's to 'write the landscape' for us,
newcomers and homeless; and a chorus
in your talk is, 'Drawing is empathy.'
This was at lunch, with wine deployed freely
for all but strong Michael, who was driver.
Outdoors, under crumbling wisteria,
crumbling our bread; the peacock's display
stalking this. Formerly a seminary,
your place's casements open on the foam
of acres of roses; on pine groves; a dome
of hill above, doodled with scrub, a line
of jet's vapour angled behind. The wine
encouraged my playful provocation,
that drawing's design. 'It's superstition,'
you said, 'sympathetic magic — the edge
Picasso had.' We accept the adage
it's based in accidents. Your mind's pliant
as your line: our elder, you're complainant
against all rigidities, including
the modernistic — cubist fracturing

you much deride. 'Every emphasis
in art means loss. Who can talk of progress?'
On our way home, I drooped in the back seat,
all windows down, struck by long shafts of heat.
Through the Blue Mountains, in raiding traffic:
less *art nouveau* forest, each year more brick.
Your feather lay lightly as a Nile boat
beside me — next thing, I saw it afloat
upon a flood tide; lifted by the draught
a stampeding truck had made. 'Plucked,' I laughed
ruefully, 'the last time.' That truck was gone,
its wheels revolving like sawmill blades, on
down the highway, in free fall, with my quill
riding the slipstream, a windsurfer's sail.
On gilt-shot air, blue smoke-burst eucalypts,
the feather's cursiveness; its catch at slips;
a rapier exploring; arabesques
above traffic behind (we loved those risks);
then, flung to the bush, defiant ensign.
I thought, 'I wish John could have seen that line.'

WINTRY DUSK, BELLINGEN

From orange grass sticks a boneyard of trees,
the night seated early under these hills,
and fibrous bushes twitch on wires of breeze —
theatrical brown flames. Evening distills
its ether, dark tree-line for sediment.
The sight of a dam's blind cataract chills.
On a last slope, the sun's emollient.

The forest's dim facade is whitely clawed.
Isolate trees step forth, wanting to speak.
Below, heavily-laddered, a dirt road;
above, aluminium, and birds stroke,
quivering like wind-pressured drops of sleet
along a screen. Quickly congealing, smoke
from a broken pillar that's red as meat.

At dusk, cellophane dimness of the world.
Two white cockatoos are raucous, over
the moon's ulcerous face, that's now revealed.
A paddock curves like a falling river,
and down through deep grass the dark fence posts ride.
Pointing everywhere, the dead trees gesture
as if they'd been in panic when they died.

EPIGRAMS

So this is the castle
of your ideals —
now show me the dungeon.

Landscape painters are the priests
and missionaries, and their art the sacrament,
of my religion.

Good is the conclusion
we draw from evil. We call good those things
that could benefit us.

Poetry is made of words, Mallarmé claimed,
which is not exact —
feelings exist as images, not as words.
(Images are the language in which we dream.)

Those who devalue pleasure
for themselves are most likely to undervalue
pain for others.

A style in art is an attitude
to experience. Looked at this way, a style can seem
ridiculous (e.g. Mondrian's).

Moral pleasure is reassurance
about the nature of human beings —
this is what we find so moving
in a work of art.

The great mystery of nature
is that it should be nothing but itself.
One has the sense of something supreme
in the most ordinary of things. . . .

The senses can mislead us,
it is true — when we rely upon
only one of them.

What one loves about nature
is its unresponsiveness —
it is, precisely,
that it 'neither cares nor knows'.

The sensory pleasures of the world
are not merely transitory —
a denigration the otherworldly have made —
but can be seen as constantly
renewed and refreshed for us.

All aesthetic judgements
are self-evident. Since they are comparative,
one need only point.

What we consider good in others
is their altruism, which we praise out of selfishness.
If we practise unselfishness ourselves,
it is for a selfish motive —
for accolade (not the least our own).

We feel nature act in us, and think
we originated the impulse,
but all of our identification
comes after the event.

Reply to Nietzsche: It is not possible
to live amongst other people
and to create one's own values.

We are all Protestants now:
all individualists
to a once-inconceivable degree.

The world, it seems, is the maximum
number of things, or of forces,
that can exist together.

Épater les bourgeois? Certainly,
but there is another complacency one mustn't
overlook. *Épater les avant-gardistes.*

SAPIENTIA LACHRIMARUM

The sound of the heat's the cicadas' note —
a drilling that forces sweat to the brow.
Or coloratura of the earth's throat

vibrates in the clearing, while eucalypts grow
silvery shafts — these pistons with their steam
about them. And neither can you follow

this intensity, and throng — there's no beam,
no mote, that's undissolved in the light's stare.
The forest ascends with a smoothness and gleam

that is oiled. It seems you're caught by a flare,
stepping into day. Withdrawn to a shack,
just this pounding shrillness, intense as the blare

of the light. The rioting of that claque
is demand to mate. As though it were rain,
one is sodden. Or, seething spear-points attack,

with rattlings. Most of the day you have lain
suffering ineptness — a full-length poultice
for sickness of spirit. The flight to Cockaigne

a chance, by late afternoon. Day's injustice
has all trees dazed as willows; but you make
the sea, in a light-struck car. It's featureless

there; the edge of grey water's laid, opaque
with light, sealed as the lip of an omelette,
on shore. Within it, like leaves that a rake

is rolling, like heavy edging of a net,
sea-wrack — which is, by thousands, the cicada.
Vaguely opaline, fabrics of the sunset;

nearby, dead panes of a yacht; in leather,
the wings that flit; coils of brown smoke, as though
away across there a city were on fire;

and these insects, once green, shown in fiasco:
they're stubbed-out, washed-up, become sodden brown.
A draggled hem. From frenzy, such overthrow;

how is a mystery. 'Not even the sun
will overstep its mark,' said Heraclitus.
That each element makes recompense was known

to Anaximander; 'for the injustice
they do, according to the ordinance
of Time.' Where the road of excess leads us

is this mess. (I have never sought guidance
of beefy, self-deluding William Blake.)
I see them abased with no exultance,

whose own complaint oversteps the mark. I walk
on rippled sand, the fallen wing of the shore,
in weird quietness. The water, engorged snake,

sluggishly winds. That sting like sweat's no more
in my head, but harmless rustlings. And these
traceries, these streamers, that the tides draw,

make me recall runnels sluicing glass; the ease
of another season. Ploughed fields under rain,
and like Epicurus's garden, the trees

rising quietly as mist, in me, in the pane,
from deep loam, where furrows end. In reverie
I see, too, how the shape of a human

is a hive for tears. Stiff or sinuously,
those roots of stumps, piled up, are warriors'
spokes, harness, ribands – all the stridency

of the mischievous and blood-coated creatures,
bogged, brought to grief. There is, if only we knew,
a land often kinder than ours, our failures'.

Also available from the
ARC PUBLICATIONS
International Poets Series

MICHAEL AUGUSTIN
A Certain Koslowski
(prose humour)
TRANSLATED FROM THE GERMAN BY MARGITT LEHBERT
ILLUSTRATED BY HARTMUT EING

ROSE AUSLÄNDER
Mother Tongue
TRANSLATED FROM THE GERMAN
BY JEAN BOASE-BEIR AND ANTHONY VIVIS

DON COLES
(Canada)
Someone has Stayed in Stockholm
NEW AND SELECTED POEMS

DINAH HAWKEN
(New Zealand)
Small Stories of Devotion

JOHN KINSELLA
(Australia)
The Undertow:
NEW AND SELECTED
The Silo:
A PASTORAL SYMPHONY

C.K. STEAD
(New Zealand)
Straw into Gold

TOMAZ SALAMUN
Homage to Hat and Uncle Guido and Eliot
SELECTED POEMS
EDITED BY CHARLES SIMIC
TRANSLATED FROM THE SLOVENE BY CHARLES SIMIC, ANSELM HOLLO ETC